# Party Poems

## Selected by John Foster

First published in the United States of America in 2008 by
**dingles & company**
P.O. Box 508
Sea Girt, New Jersey 08750

First Printing

Website: www.dingles.com

E-mail: info@dingles.com

**Library of Congress Catalog Card No.:** 2007907138

**ISBN:** 978-1-59646-582-4 (library binding)
978-1-59646-583-1 (paperback)

© Oxford University Press
This U.S. edition of *Party Poems*, originally published in English in 2004, is published by arrangement with Oxford University Press.

*Acknowledgments*
The editor and publisher wish to thank the following who have kindly given permission for the use of copyright material:

Clare Bevan for "I Want a Balloon", © Clare Bevan 2004
Andrew Collett for "Jelly", © Andrew Collett 2004
John Foster for "Birthday Cake", © John Foster 2004
Roger Stevens for "Party Hats", © Roger Stevens 2004

*Illustrations by*
Beccy Blake; Basia Bogdanowicz c/o Linda Rogers Associates;
Alison Carney; Louise Gardner

Printed in China

# Birthday Cake

Light the candles.
Get ready to blow.

# One, two, three,
# and out they go!

*John Foster*

# I Want a Balloon

I want a balloon
to take away.
I want a balloon.
I want one today.

I'll stamp and I'll shout,
and I will not stop.
I WANT A BALLOON!

I've got one! POP!!!!

*Clare Bevan*

# Party Hats

Yellow hat, blue hat, green hat, red—
I've got a party hat on my head.

Yellow hat, green hat, red hat, blue—
even the hamster has one, too!

*Roger Stevens*

9

# Jelly

Jelly on my head,
jelly on the door,
jelly on the wall,
jelly on the floor.

Jelly in my belly.
Can I have some more?

*Andrew Collett*

# Out and About Poems

## Selected by John Foster

First published in the United States of America in 2008 by
**dingles & company**
P.O. Box 508
Sea Girt, New Jersey 08750

First Printing

Website: www.dingles.com

E-mail: info@dingles.com

**Library of Congress Catalog Card No.:** 2007907138

**ISBN:** 978-1-59646-582-4 (library binding)
      978-1-59646-583-1 (paperback)

© Oxford University Press
This U.S. edition of *Out and About Poems*, originally published in English in 2004, is published by arrangement with Oxford University Press.

*Acknowledgments*
The editor and publisher wish to thank the following who have kindly given permission for the use of copyright material:

Andrew Collett for "Skip", © Andrew Collett 2004
John Foster for "At the Seaside", "The Fair" and "You Can't Catch Me"
© John Foster 2004

*Illustrations by*
Rebecca Archer; Teri Gower c/o Malcolm Sherman Associates;
Paula Knight; Kathy Taggart

Printed in China

# The Fair

I went to the fair.
I went on a train.
I went on a bus.
I went on a plane.

I went on a horse.
I won a brown bear.

I had lots of fun
when I went to the fair.

*John Foster*

# At the Seaside

We went in the sea.
We had a good swim.
Tim splashed me.
I splashed him.

We dug in the sand.
We dug all day.

We made a big sand castle.
The sea washed it away.

*John Foster*

# Skip!

One skip, two skip,
three skip, four,
five skip, six skip,
seven skip, more!

Eight skip, nine skip,
ten skip, hop –
skip skip, skip skip,
skip skip, STOP!

*Andrew Collett*

# You Can't Catch Me

Run around the swing.
Run around the tree.
Run around the slide.
You can't catch me!

*John Foster*